RelationShift

RelationShift

By: LaQuonne Holden

XULON PRESS ELITE

Xulon Press Elite
2301 Lucien Way #415
Maitland, FL 32751
407.339.4217
www.xulonpress.com

© 2019 by LaQuonne Holden

All rights reserved solely by the author. The author guarantees all contents are original and do not infringe upon the legal rights of any other person or work. No part of this book may be reproduced in any form without the permission of the author. The views expressed in this book are not necessarily those of the publisher.

Unless otherwise indicated, Scripture quotations taken from the Holy Bible, New International Version (NIV). Copyright © 1973, 1978, 1984, 2011 by Biblica, Inc.™. Used by permission. All rights reserved.

Scripture quotations taken from the New King James Version (NKJV). Copyright © 1982 by Thomas Nelson, Inc. Used by permission. All rights reserved.

Scripture quotations taken from the Holy Bible, New Living Translation (NLT). Copyright ©1996, 2004, 2007 by Tyndale House Foundation. Used by permission of Tyndale House Publishers, Inc.

Scripture quotations taken from the Amplified Bible (AMP). Copyright © 1954, 1958, 1962, 1964, 1965, 1987 by The Lockman Foundation. Used by permission. All rights reserved.

Scripture quotations taken from The Message (MSG). Copyright © 1993, 1994, 1995, 1996, 2000, 2001, 2002. Used by permission of NavPress Publishing Group. Used by permission. All rights reserved.

Printed in the United States of America.

ISBN-13: 978-1-54566-499-5

CONTENTS

ACKNOWLEDGMENTS

With Special Thanks:

To my amazing wife, Jacinta Holden, whose immeasurable love made this book possible.

To my spiritual parents, Pastor Dharius and Lady Shameka Daniels, who stabilizes and guides my soul.

To my father Tyrone and mother Gwen, who raised me with values that make a difference.

To my other parents, Glenn and Kulah, whose support helps me to move forward.

To my brother Tyrone (Zok), whose been a catalyst throughout my life.

To my other brother, Montel, who inspired me to move beyond what is comfortable.

To my creative specialists, Lamar Harvey and Shalondie Stephen, for your commitment, coordination, and collaboration to completion.

To my CrossLife Church family, who first received the RelationShift message with openness.

To the Life team, for your unwavering support, commitment, encouragement, prayers, and push.

To the hosts of pastors, mentors, extended family, and friends, who support and encourage me.

To the Xulon Press family, who believed in and supported this message through your services.

PREFACE

Do you need to shift your relationships? What's the purpose of a relationship? Before you can answer these questions or determine how to manage your relationships, you must be clear on what a relationship's purpose is in your life. Author LaQuonne Holden offers a unique perspective to bring clarity on the matter that produces fruitful relationships on purpose. He draws from a wellspring of wisdom gained through lessons learned from personal experiences and revelatory insight to help you clearly determine how to assess where a shift should take place in your relationships. Change doesn't happen until something else happens. When you have a shift in your relationship, your relationship can function on another level. A person's life will function at the level of his/her most authentic relationships and deepest connections; therefore, choose wisely who you closely relate with.

Relationships are essential for where you are now and where you desire to go. LaQuonne firmly believes that your relationships have the ability to stall you or drive you forward, as he metaphorically likens relationships to a method of transportation in your life. He states that like a car when you're in the wrong gear, it doesn't run correctly; it may stall on you and cut off without further warning. The same applies to your relationships in life, so make sure that you're in the right gear to move forward! This book will help you clearly understand the purpose of right relationships and how to determine the right people in your life.

When you can define where your relationship is, you can determine where the shift can be made! As you walk through the pages of this book, you will clearly come to discover the answer to this question in your relationships: Is it time for your RelationShift?

CHAPTER 1

What Is IT?

Every relationship will move at the speed of trust, which means that connections with others will grow and develop at the pace where trust has been established. What defines your relationships? I believe that before you can adequately answer this question, you must first be clear on what a relationship is defined as. What is a relationship? I believe that a relationship is the way that two or more people are connected to, regard, and behave toward one another. Once you define your relationships, you can determine how you should manage them.

Relationship management, in essence, is the supervision or maintenance of relationships, which I believe is an important responsibility to manage; regardless of the type of relationship that one has with another. The purpose and core value of this book is to bring clarity through the perspective to produce fruitful relationships on purpose.

Through this book, I pray you are able to clearly know the heart of God concerning the relationships you may have in your life. This is not an attempt to express all that I believe or have come to experience in my relationships with people, but to offer my narrative from a biblical perspective based on many of my experiences in defining relationships throughout my life. I believe that if I were to ask ten people what a relationship is or means to them, I would argue that the majority would indicate and emphasize the type of relationship they have rather than actually defining what a relationship really is, regardless of the type of relationship that one has with another. The common cause of most relationships stems from the place of need it resides in; which, in turn, results in the effects of people entering and managing relationships from the basis of a need or needs being met by a person or people without first establishing a clear understanding of what a relationship is and how one should approach the matter of relationship. The question that must be asked is, "What happens to the relationship when the need has been met?"

In the following chapters, I will share the revelatory insight I have gained through learned experiences from relationships that failed and those that flourished. In the end, I have come to know that no matter what type of relationship one has with another, every right relationship in your life is two-fold and should never be one-sided, as the goal of any relationship should be to benefit one another. Through failures and successes throughout my relationships in life, I am able to enter and manage relationships better because of the lessons I have learned along the way. I desire to offer you an opportunity to learn from my experiences and gain insight in an effort to help you avoid learning some lessons the hard way as you enter and manage your relationships in life. How you enter a relationship will affect how you begin to manage it. Lastly, it is worth noting that I believe no person was created to live life alone and before your life is over, you will need to trust someone to help you in life as you live life. As you journey to read the path that I have walked with people, never lose sight of the fact that every relationship moves at the speed of trust.

After you define your relationship, you can determine the shift within the relationship. When this becomes known, you can understand why the title of this book is RelationShift and how this perspective applies to most relationships that you will have in your life. Before we can adequately assess what a RelationShift is, we must accurately define what a shift means. I believe that a shift represents movement from one place to another or some change in position or direction. Your relationships will move in one direction or another, which can cause you to be in another position and discover another tendency within that relationship.

Relationships will take you somewhere, so the most essential thing is to know how to manage a relationship as it shifts in your life. As we journey ahead in the pages and chapters to come, you will come to know where the shift is or should be in your relationship. You can't accurately assess where a relationship is until you can accurately define what a relationship is. Journey with me through perspectives and principles that I believe will help you determine the state of your relationships and give you the clear understanding to assess what your RelationShift is.

Another aspect of defining a relationship can be clearly seen in a relational connection that gives and adds value to you. In every healthy relationship, there should be a healthy level of sacrifice from those in the relationship. As a disclaimer to this thought, as it pertains to this chapter, let me frame it this way using an analogy of transportation: If a relationship isn't giving you the fuel to move forward in your life, the connection is diminishing the tread wear of your life. This prohibits your purpose and becomes the hindrance to you moving where you're supposed to be, because the end result is that the relationship will wear you out. You should be willing to give to people the way that you want others to give to you.

The essence of God's preference for our relationship with Him is based on two critical components that express the level of our relationship with Him and enable us to clearly see His best in our lives: convicted and committed relationships based on the relationship law of sacrifice.

Is your relationship giving you what you need for support?

Relationships challenge and call us away from selfishness and self-focus into an attitude of sacrifice, selflessness, and service to others. In a relational connection, it's not always about what your relationship can do for you but what you can do for your relationship.

When we think about what we can do for others instead of what they can do for us, we get to the very heart of healthy, successful relationships. One of the immutable laws of relationships is the law of sacrifice, which means everyone involved must enter into and remain in a relationship with a willingness to give, not to take. Both parties should be willing to sacrifice for each other and the relationship as a whole.

The only things we should never sacrifice in a relationship are integrity, character, biblical principles, and our walks with God. In truly healthy relationships, people will not ask us to sacrifice such significant aspects of our lives but will appreciate and honor them. Aside from these priorities, everything else is eligible to be placed on the altar of sacrifice.

Sacrifice is something God has demonstrated personally and something He requires of us for healthy relationships. It is never easy or pleasant because certain enemies of sacrifice are wired into human nature and are constantly pulling us to side with them. There are two specific enemies we must defeat if we are going to sacrifice in ways that honor God and benefit our relationships: comfort and convenience.

Do you have a relationship based on comfort? When people become comfortable with others, they develop a sense of familiarity that can easily breed neglect, lassitude, and indifference. This causes disregard of others and taking them for granted, which leads to taking undue liberties in the relationship and causing instances of disrespect that become major problems over time.

Is your relationship based on convenience? The other enemy of sacrifice, an accomplice to the trap of comfort, is the snare of convenience. In order to have healthy, biblical relationships, we must discard the idea of convenience because godly relationships have nothing to do with whether they are convenient or not. They require investments of time, energy, and resources based on a commitment, rather than a convenience, to give.

If your relationships are going to become anything valuable and sustaining, sacrifice will be necessary. It is also worth sharing that there is a correlation between sacrifice and something being sustained through the sacrifice, especially in the context of relationships. In the fulfillment of a relationship that reciprocates, gives, and adds value, it will result in a strong and stable connection. Relationships have to be maintained with steady investments of time and interaction. Are you ready to define your relationships?

Let's journey together as we look to discover where your RelationShift can take place.

CHAPTER 2

Relate to IT!

I believe that in the beginning, God created us for relationship and we are crafted to relate to Him and to others. When we miss out on experiencing relationships, we're missing the core reason for which God put us on this planet. A life without connection may be a less complex life, but it is also a life of emptiness. Simply put, we need to relate to others, and in this chapter, I want us to come to the conclusion that answers the next question.

How do you relate in your relationships? What does relate mean to you in the context of a relationship? One of the meanings of relate that I believe is applicable to a relationship is being able to indicate the connection with something else. This means that when you have discovered and determined for yourself what a relationship is, you have the framework to assist yourself in learning what it means to relate to others in relationships.

In order to relate to someone else, for the benefit of connection in a relationship, it has been from my experience and evaluation that the best way to view any relationship is to see it through the lens of how you relate to yourself first. You should always remember that the purpose of relationship is to encounter, experience, and embrace the exchange of knowing and sharing in the life of another person. We must ask ourselves this question when it comes to our relationships with others: "Can I relate with another differently than how I relate to myself?" This perspective allows you to see your relationships differently because it is my belief that it is extremely difficult, or nearly impossible, to relate to others in a way that you don't relate to yourself. For example, if you are not honest with yourself, how can you relate to others honestly? When it comes to the principle of relating to others in relationships, be clear that it starts with you. How you see others is often a reflection of how you see yourself, as the ability to relate to another is the catalyst for connection in any relationship. Can you relate to it?

As you begin to understand what it means to relate to others, beginning with yourself, be assured that your relationship with someone else will never reach a level beyond the scope of the level you are able to see yourself. This principle is found in the Bible passage of Isaiah 6, where we can catch a glimpse of what it means to relate and connect for the purpose of relationship that begins with how we view ourselves first. In short paraphrase, we see that the prophet Isaiah had a vision of the Lord, that he desired to connect with after seeing the beauty of who the Lord was in the vision, but it caused him to immediately see himself as not so beautiful, and it humbled him deeply. Despite the current place where life may have you, the question is, "Can you look beyond where you are and have the vision to see the beauty of what the Lord has already planned, purposed, and provided for you; to help shift your focus from being stuck in the past?" Can you relate to it?

The truth of the matter from Isaiah 6 is that there are many other qualities we can learn and apply to our lives and relationships with others. The purpose of this book is to help you clearly see that the course and quality of your life is interconnected with the relationships in your life. Before we continue forward past this chapter, and journey further on this walk to discover and determine our RelationShift, allow me to share with you a simple but profound truth that I have personally learned, embraced, and still apply in my life in regards to relating to others in a relationship.

For me, I believe that as you look outside of yourself, through the lens of your relationship with God, you will gain insight that allows you to look within yourself through the lens of how the Lord sees you. This will enable and empower you to not only connect but relate going forward with another, as you look out for the benefit of others. You can see another person for who he/she appears to be in nature or character by watching and looking at a person, because you receive and accept others based on how you perceive them. Your intent should be to see your relationship in the light of the Lord in connection to how you see yourself. You can always relate to others as you engage to connect by looking and watching. Can you relate to it?

When it comes to relating to others and maintaining relationships with people, we must come to understand that it will require a mental fortitude and a healthy way of thinking through the many complexities often associated with consistently developing any relationship. Relationship is the one area where I believe we must put this principle into practice. It has been said, and it has become known, that our greatest joys and greatest pains come from relationships. Some life events bring great joy, such as weddings, births, and reunions, whereas other life events like divorce, funerals, and disagreements can be the source of our greatest pain at times. The truth is that people are not perfect, making trouble inevitable because life is both a balance and mixture of pleasure and pain.

The question we must consider is this: Is your relationship established and guided by your heart or your head? Dr. Dharius Daniels asserts in his book, *RePresent Jesus (2014)*, that:

"when relationships are led by people's hearts instead of their heads, challenges will ensue as it becomes difficult to relate to people in this manner. He also states that emotional intelligence affects our relational intelligence; which means that if we live by how we feel concerning people and allow our feelings to drive our interactions, regarding who can come into our lives and who can leave our lives, we will lose the value of our ability to use our minds in relating to others."

We will be able to better relate to other people when we understand that relationships possess the ability to change our lives. This has been my belief for many years, as I believe that God's greatest source of blessing is found in those we are in relationship with. On the contrary, our greatest source of frustration can also come through our relationships. Relationships have proven over time that they are consequential; therefore, we should choose wisely in who we attempt to connect and relate to in life. Proverbs 13:20 teaches us that we can obtain wisdom just by walking with wise people. While this is true, the same applies if we relate and walk with people who entertain foolishness. It is quite possible for people to become products of a bad environment even if they are sincerely good people. Look at this way: Just because people are not always bad doesn't mean that those people can't be bad for you, as bad company corrupts good character. How do you relate in your relationships?

CHAPTER 3

Authenticate IT!

Now that you have a clearer understanding of what a relationship is and an awareness as to how you relate to others, you must become alert on assessing your authentic and superficial relationships. This chapter is essential, and I believe it will serve you in helping you to discover, discern, and determine where your RelationShift with another should occur. As mentioned earlier, the course and quality of your life is intertwined with the relationships in your life; this means that priority must be given and a premium must be placed on you evaluating your relationships to clearly know if your relationship is authentic or superficial, friend or foe, because it becomes vital to helping or hurting you in the meantime.

The goal of this chapter is to give you practical principles that will aid you in your assessment of others through the view of your values and the lens of how you identify in life to authenticate true relationships and separate from false and superficial relationships. This is the essence of your RelationShift, as real relationships move you forward while false connections hold you back.

Before you can accurately attempt to authenticate any relationship, you should first know what authenticate means. In a relationship context, I believe that authenticate means to prove what is genuine and validate one's identity. I believe the purpose of this place in your journey with me is to walk in wisdom concerning the people you are connected to in your life. As I reflect over the course of my life and align the actions and events that occurred in various stages of my life, I can clearly see the need to authenticate every relationship moving forward.

As you come to align your life with a principle found in God's Word, let this truth connect with you as you relate to it so that it can potentially protect you from something that you may not have to go through or experience personally. I believe that this principle is not only life-applicable, but it is life-altering for greater perspective, as it provides the way to walk on the road of connectedness for your relationships. To authenticate your relationship, you must first be true to yourself. When you remain true to yourself, you can expect truth from others. If you want to be trusted, be honest. If you want to be honest, be true. If you want to be true, be yourself. Ask yourself this question in every relationship to begin the authentication process, "What do I bring to the table?" In any relationship, something good or bad will be brought to your life and every relationship moves at the speed of the trust established over a period of time.

This is important to know and understand because many people become the recipients of wrong relationships due to a love for people misplaced with a trust of people. We should love everyone, but our trust should always be earned. Ask yourself this question: "Am I entrusting my life to someone who hasn't earned it?" The mismanagement or mishandling of the truth can bring detrimental results that hinder our destinies. The place where these principles are discovered is seen through the perspective of God's Word; over different passages that speak of events occurring in the lives of some of Jesus's disciples who had brotherly relationships with each other, potentially on different levels. John tells us in 1 John 4:11 (paraphrase mine) to not put our trust in every person, as their nature is unknown at first; but to prove them over a period of time that allows the character, intent, and nature of that individual to determine if they are considered trustworthy by the standard of the Lord. In practical terms, look at this way; don't put your trust in any relationship that hasn't been proven. Give yourself adequate time to know who you are dealing with before you share the treasure of your life, which is hidden for a reason from others. In the school of relationship, class is always in session; just pay attention because when the test is given, you don't want to fail with a grade of pain!

Whatever you purpose to do in your life will demand you know the authenticity of the person you may connect and relate to in a relationship. In the book of Joshua, chapter 5, as he nears Jericho, the first thing he demanded to know, was who came in front of him or appeared into his life while he was moving toward the mission that God had given him, and he asked this question, "are you friend or foe?" (Josh. 5:13 NLT). When someone appears in your life as you move forward, it should drive you to first authenticate by determining who a person is, so you can better discern between friend or foe.

The truth of this principle is that every relationship will either be a blessing (friend) or a lesson (foe) in your life. The process we must undergo to authenticate our relationships should prompt us to be asking these questions: "Are you adding value or taking away from life? Are you helping me to serve my purpose or hindering me and keeping me stuck in the past?" These are essential questions to consider in your evaluation and examination of authenticating your relationships. Another principle to help you authenticate relationships is found in the book of 1 John 2:19 (AMP; paraphrase mine) that says there are times in our lives where a RelationShift is required because of the season we are living in at that time. Know this; your season of life will demand separation from certain people, because separation is the pruning of God to rid your life of anyone who hinders your obedience in following Him.

A lack of obedience becomes the obstacle that prohibits purpose. It may look like your overall circle of people in life decreases in natural size but be assured that this authentication process causes an increase in total value for your relationships. I believe that you don't need a large entourage close to you but just the loyalty from the right few to push you beyond where you are now. This is the reward that is seen from relationship authentication. The harsh truth is that everyone who comes into your life doesn't care about your purpose the way that you do. To place your promise in the hands of someone who doesn't care about your purpose is the same as placing your potential in the grave.

Never give someone else the power to destroy what is inside of you, because he/she hasn't earned the right to it. Authenticating your relationship allows you to see who is loyal to you and can be trusted by you. Don't trust your life permanently to someone who is temporarily loyal for a season. You need to assess your relationship over time to notice a pattern develop of consistency. John 15:14 shows us that love is proved by consistent actions. Authentication in your relationship is clearly determined through consistency. While life is full of change, this doesn't always mean that loyalty should always change too. I have learned in my life that some people aren't loyal to you; they are loyal to their need of you. Once their needs change, so does their loyalty. Encourage yourself with the understanding of this principle: The only people you owe your loyalty to are those who never make you question theirs. Is it time to shift the way you connect in relationships with people? What good is connecting in a relationship if it isn't a right relationship for you?

When it comes to authenticating your relationship, another aspect that must be considered is assessing the level of communication in the relationship. While every relationship moves at the speed of trust, I believe it also moves at the speed of communication. You need trust and communication in your relationship to grow in the way you are going. In your relationships with people, you should know some things and be willing to share some things as you can't know or share without communication.

Communication is vital in every relationship, whether in a marriage, friendship, partnership, etc. You should communicate thoroughly, properly, and timely. For illustrative purposes, to paint a picture of this principle in the context of relationship, think about it like this: When you are driving a car and need to shift lanes or your position on the highway, the signal light communicates to other drivers your next move. The brake light tells them that you are stopping or slowing down. Without effective communication, you will cause accidents; accidents on the road to where you are going; accidents in life. Most accidents can be avoided if there was proper communication from all involved. Your ability to communicate will be the key to your relationship moving at a top speed without experiencing further delays to where you want to be.

For your relationship to move at top speed, it's essential for you to be thorough in communicating the details about where you are going and what is going on in your relationship. When you neglect to communicate thoroughly with one another, the results can be catastrophic. When you know you are in a relationship with someone, you have to share something. If your relationship is in a standstill, check to see if there were signals warning you beforehand. In the school of relationships, class is always in session so we must pay attention. Is there communication in your relationship?

Another principle that plays out in our lives when we embrace authenticating our relationships is to know the difference of those relationships that prove authenticity from the relationships that prove to be superficial. In the Bible, Jesus had two disciples (Peter and Judas) who followed Him closely for three years and did something to Him as the result of temptation where they both failed to resist when the opportunity arose. Loyalty proves itself to be loyal in the face of temptation and opportunity. The greatest assessment to authenticate your relationships is to discover not what happens when you are present but what takes place in your absence. Superficial relationships will expose themselves in the face of anything that appears to be a greater opportunity to get ahead of you, because the people fail to see the true value of you.

The difference between both events that happened in the lives of Peter and Judas was that Peter seemingly had a bad day, whereas Judas had a bad heart.

There is no relationship that is perfect, but every relationship should serve a purpose. Authentic relationships will last longer than a mistake, see you past a season, pray with you in pain, commit to your cause, partner with you for purpose, invest into your inheritance, not seek to terminate your trust through betrayal for personal gain, and last long enough to establish a legacy with you.

CHAPTER 4

Is IT Credible?

Is your relationship credible? To assess your relationship for credibility and to answer this question, you must understand what credible means in the context of relationship. I believe that credible relationships indicate a strong, convincing connection and with the belief that the relationship will be successful for all involved. With this, now ask yourself the question: Is my relationship convincing and capable of being a successful relationship?

Dr. Stephen Covey refers to four cores of credibility when it comes to relationship trust, which I want to use and explore in the context for this chapter on helping you to assess your relationship credibility. The fact is that every relationship moves at the speed of trust, and trust is essential to grow any relationship, being that when trust is established, it builds relational equity. Relationship equity can only increase when there is relationship credibility. The credibility of a relationship requires a strong core to support and sustain the building of that relationship. As we look at credibility in the context of relationship, it boils down to two simple questions:

1. Do I trust myself?
2. Am I someone who others can trust?

Once you are able to answer these questions, the process of becoming aware of credibility comes into focus, as you come to see the four cores that are necessary to building relationship credibility. The four cores to establish relationship credibility are:

1. Integrity (character)
2. Intent (character)
3. Capabilities (competency)
4. Results (competency)

Integrity and intent are character cores, whereas capabilities and results are competency cores. All four of these cores are required for credibility. For practical application purposes, let's look at it this way: If a person of integrity does not produce results, this person is not credible. If someone is not credible, he/she is not trustworthy.

When we truly understand these four cores, we will be able to better identify the condition of our relationship credibility with people as a whole. The first core is integrity. Most trust problems are issues of integrity. I believe that integrity is more than honesty alone and consists of other virtues such as motive, intent, and truth.

Congruency is when one acts according to his values; it is when there is no gap between what one intends to do and what one actually does in a relationship. I believe that humility is the ability to look out for the good of others, in addition to what is good for you. I say this because I have learned in my life that a person of humility is more concerned about what is right than about being right, about acting on good ideas than about having the ideas, about embracing new truth than defending an old position, about building team than elevating self, about recognizing contribution than receiving it. Courage is the ability to do the right thing, even when it may be difficult; it is when you do what you know is right regardless of the possible consequences against you.

The second core is intent. Intent springs from our character and is part of our value system. It is how we know we should act. This can be broken down to three things: Motive, agenda, and behavior.

Motive is why you do what you do. The best motive in building trust is genuinely caring about people. If you don't care and have no desire to care, be honest and let people know you don't care. If you don't care but want to care, start to care about things; often, the feelings will follow the actions. Agenda stems from our motives. The best agenda is honestly seeking what is good for others. Notice that your agenda is much more than wanting what is good for others but seeking what is good for others. Behavior is putting your agenda into practice; it is what we do based upon what we intend to do and what we are actively seeking. Behavior is where the rubber meets the road and is important because it is what people see and judge. Telling someone you love him/her is important but showing the person you love him/her is essential.

To improve the core of our intent, here are my suggestions:

1. Assess your motives.
2. Make known your intent.
3. Choose what is right based on biblical truth.

The third core is capabilities. Capabilities consist of the talents, skills, knowledge, capacities, and abilities we have that enable us to perform with excellence. I believe that the depth of our capabilities is often expressed through our talents, attitude, skills, knowledge, and style. Talents are the things we naturally do well and are the things we usually love to do. Your attitude is how you see things; it is how we are inside. Skills are the things you have learned to do well. It is easy to get so comfortable with our skills that we never fulfill our talents. I believe that talent is a deeper well than skill.

Knowledge is what you know and continue to learn, while style is your unique way of doing things. It involves your personality. Practically, we must ask ourselves how can we increase our capabilities? I suggest that first, identify your strengths and your passions.

Second, remain relevant by continually increasing your knowledge and improving your skills. Third, know where you are going. The people you lead will follow if you know where you are going.

The fourth core is results. The truth is that people don't trust people who don't deliver with results. Results are the deliverables; they are what you contribute to something. You can't hide from your results because when the results are absent, credibility becomes missing as well. There are three areas of results people look at to judge your credibility. First, your past results: what you have proven you can do. Second, your current results: what you are contributing right now. Third, your potential results: what people anticipate you will accomplish in the future which is your perceived potential.

Perhaps you're wondering as to how to improve your results. First, take responsibility for results, not activity. Second, expect to achieve your goals. Assume you will be successful, and this assumption will translate into action. Third, finish strong, because any result is about an ability to finish. In the context of relationship, your result is often found in your ability to follow up and follow through. Just because a relationship started together doesn't guarantee that it will end up together. It's not about how something starts; it's about how it finishes.

A final principle I want to share that I believe is essential to establishing relationship credibility is to understand that trust is predicated on consistent behavior. Any relationship that is not tested is a relationship that cannot be trusted. If a relationship cannot be trusted, it will not have any relational equity. To establish relationship credibility, we need to be clear on the behaviors that result in trust.

Relationship trust is all about consistent behavior. People judge us on behavior, not intent. People can't see our hearts, but they can see our behavior. Creating and developing relationship credibility is essentially about establishing relationship equity. This happens in relationships when you are able to build relationship trust accounts. There are several keys to making trust accounts. The fastest way to build a trust account is to stop making withdrawals, as you have to be aware that withdrawals are bigger than deposits. Each trust account is unique. There are two ways of viewing a trust account: your way and their way. A deposit in one person's account may be a withdrawal from another person's account.

Let's look at different relationship behaviors that are able to build trust, which can establish credibility. In every relationship, there will be a form of behavior that builds credibility or destroys it. To assess relationship credibility, consider how you identify with these behaviors:

1. Real Talk

Say what is on your mind. Don't hide your agenda. When we talk straight, we tell the truth and leave the right impression. This creates a trust tax. This causes relationship speed to go down and relationship costs to go up. Straight talk needs to be paired with tact, for there is no excuse for being so blunt that you hurt feelings and destroy relationships. Tact is a skill that can be learned and when coupled with straight talk, it will build relationship trust.

2. Respect

The principle behind demonstrating respect is the value of the individual. The behavior is acting out the Golden Rule, and almost every culture and religion recognizes the value of the Golden Rule. We should treat people the way we want to be treated. Our actions should show we care and should be sincere. Respect is demonstrated in the little things we do daily.

3. Transparency

Tell the truth in a way that can be verified. Transparency is based on principles of honesty, openness, integrity, and authenticity. It is based on doing things in the open where all can see. Part of transparency is sharing information. If ever in question, err on the side of disclosure.

4. Right Wrongs

To right a wrong is much more than apologizing; it involves making restitution. It is the principle of going the extra mile. Some will justify their wrongful behavior while others will try covering up their misdeeds. Both of these attempts will not only fail to make deposits in trust accounts but are certain to make substantial withdrawals from the relationship.

5. Loyalty

There are many ways to show loyalty. First, give credit to others. Giving credit to others is the right thing to do. It will foster an environment where people are encouraged to be creative and innovative. It will increase trust and have a direct impact on the health of the relationship. Second, speak about others as if they were present. Some people think it builds relationships to talk about others, but the opposite is true. Talking about others behind their backs will decrease trust with others.

6. Results

The fastest way to build trust with someone is to deliver results. Results give you instant credibility and trust. Delivering results is based on competence because it is a behavior that is produced from responsibility, accountability, and performance. Results change people, establish trust in new relationships, and restore trust that has been lost due to lack of competence.

7. Improvement

In today's ever-changing environment, one must continue to improve or become obsolete. You cannot learn a skill and ride that one skill for thirty years; you have to constantly be improving. When others see you continually learning and adapting to change, they become more confident in your ability. Be careful not to become a life-long learner who does not produce, or one who sees only one way to improve self and others. Practical ways to improve in your relationship are to seek feedback from those around you and to learn from your mistakes.

8. Face Reality

We cannot close our eyes to the tough realities we face. If we are honest about the difficult issues and are addressing them head-on, people will trust us. We have to avoid the temptation to avoid reality or act as if we are addressing the difficult issues while we are actually evading them.

9. Clarify Expectations

When expectations are not clearly defined up front, relationship trust and speed both go down. A lot of time is wasted due to the individuals in the relationship not clearly defining expectations. Failure to clarify expectations leaves people guessing.

10. Accountability

People build trust by first holding themselves accountable, then holding others accountable. Holding yourself accountable includes taking responsibility for bad results. It is often our natural response to blame others for failure. When we fail, we need to look in the mirror. Holding others accountable allows others to feel good about where they are and what they are doing in the relationship.

11. Listening

Listening before prescribing advice builds trust. Trying to give advice before knowing all the facts is a waste of time and simply not fair. You need to be careful not to learn the mechanics of listening and leave the impression you are listening when you're really not. Remember that communication is more than just words, so you will have to listen to nonverbal messages as well. If a person is displaying a high level of emotion, he/she doesn't feel understood. Keep listening. Also, a person is not likely to ask for advice until he/she feels you understand all the pertinent information. Don't give advice too early but take time to intently listen.

12. Commitment

When you make a commitment, you build hope. When you keep a commitment, you build trust. Be careful when making commitments; make only the commitments you can keep and don't be vague when making commitments. There are implicit and explicit commitments and violating either is a huge withdrawal from the relationship trust account. Be aware of the expectations to a commitment.

13. Trust

This behavior helps you to become a trusting person. We should extend trust to those who have earned it. Be willing to extend trust to those who are still earning it. Be wise in extending trust to those who have not exemplified a character worth trusting.

CHAPTER 5

Is IT Healthy?

When a relationship is credible, the question that still needs to be answered is, is this relationship healthy? What is the health of your relationship? Is this person capable of building a healthy relationship? While these are questions that necessitate answers, there are some variables that must be considered that I believe are standard in relating to others. In a social age where digital media influences connection on a surface and shallow level, similar personalities, common goals, dreams, and mere attraction alone do not substantiate relationship wellness.

The truth is that relationship wellness cannot be lessened to just how someone makes you feel, because something that feels good to you does not mean that something is good for you. Your relationship should not be built on false pretenses or include pockets of dishonesty or disrespect on any level. The associations that will take you to the next level in your life have to be pure, solid, deep, and full of integrity, as it establishes relationship credibility as shared in the previous chapter.

I believe that many people have missed out on relationship wellness, with a benefit to their lives, because they were not willing to establish the right relationship with the right people in the right way. Cultivating right and healthy relationships with people requires a combination of attitudes and actions that lead to relational health and, ultimately, to personal growth and advancement.

Scripture provides us a tremendous example of two people who developed and sustained a healthy relationship.

In 1 Kings 19 and 2 Kings 2, we see that the young prophet Elisha wants to establish a relationship with the older and more experienced prophet Elijah. This relationship will be critical to Elisha's future, as he will end up being blessed in extraordinary ways because of Elijah.

During the course of his ministry, the younger Elisha performs twice as many miracles as the Elijah and enjoys the double portion he requests. This relationship that so blesses Elisha's life requires several things of him: commitment and respect, desiring the best for his mentor, an active involvement in something positive, a capacity for healthy relationship, a willingness to deal with unpleasant situations, and the willingness to sacrifice for something new and different. The relationships that will raise your life to a new level and drive you into great blessings will require some investments of you.

Second Kings 2:9-10 (NLT) says:

> Elijah said to Elisha, "Tell me what I can do for you before I am taken away." And Elisha replied, "Please let me inherit a double share of your spirit and become your successor. You have asked a difficult thing," Elijah replied. "If you see me when I am taken from you, then you will get your request. But if not, then you won't."

Who wants to share in your success? There is no sharing in the success of anyone without a cost. The healthy relationships in your life will involve a significant element of commitment. Can you remain in a relationship when doing so is easy and when it is grueling? It will require the refusal to abandon or forsake a friend, spouse, family member, or colleague in the moments when you really want to run from the relationship. While I don't recommend, and will never recommend, staying in a relationship that is abusive, I do understand that all relationships have seasons of difficulty. In these instances, the question you must ask yourself when it comes to your relationship is, is this relationship a difficulty or a detriment? One mark of a healthy association is the ability to stay committed through tough times.

Great relationships aren't built on good times alone, and they don't develop quickly. They take time, and that time needs to include challenges because challenges are incubators for growth, strength, and trust. A substantive, healthy relationship will weather storms and trials, and it will stand strong over a long period of time because everyone involved is committed. I have come to learn in my life that sometimes people stay committed in relationships for the wrong reasons. They know they can benefit from another person, so they contrive a false kind of loyalty designed to get them what they want. This is both wrong and unhealthy. In a healthy relationship, commitment is based on respect. A truth about great relationships is that one person cannot disrespect another and also expect to receive from that person. Disrespect, dishonor, and disregard have ways of canceling any potential benefits of a personal or professional association. The only way to receive from people is to respect them.

Great relationships will always require something of you. What are some general criteria when assessing relationship wellness?

1. Commitment and Respect (proven by your loyalty and actions)
2. Celebrates and Desires the Best (celebrate your changes and elevation in your life)
3. Engaged and Expectant (involved with what happens and expects the best for you)
4. Demonstrates and Interacts (capacity to handle much and share in the responsibility)

5. Wrestles and Works (doesn't mind getting his/her hands dirty with you)
6. Willingness and Available (sacrifices for new, different, and better than before)

Do you want what you've always had, or are you open to the potential of something new?

Every relationship that is tested is a relationship that can be trusted. Whatever and whoever you come into agreement with, you must remain committed to in relationship. Your significant sacrifices and separation from your past history are the keys to embracing your future, pressing into your purpose, and driving toward your destiny. The opportunities to move ahead in life from right and healthy relationships will always come with a cost and a price from your life.

When God wants to do something tremendous in your life, He will always use a word and a person, just as He always has. The question is, when that word comes to you and when that person enters your life, will you leave behind everything old and move into something new and great? Healthy relationships always come with benefits that add immeasurable value to your life.

Is your relationship healthy? Past history is not the guarantee for future connection. Don't continue riding with those that only relate with your history but drive with those that can actually see your destiny. Carrying people in your life the wrong way will hinder your destiny and potentially prohibit your purpose. Is helping them hurting you?

There is a relationship law that I believe is in place to help govern your soul, so that you can continue to guard your heart because from this place produces the other issues of your life. It's hard to accelerate to the next level in life if you're holding onto people, places, and things you need to let go of. Do you believe that it is possible to have a healthy relationship with an unhealthy person or people?

No relationship is perfect, but a great relationship is progressive. As long as growth happens, movement together can happen. When you grow forward, you can go forward. Are you willing to shift from only familiar relationships to accelerate into what's purposed concerning you? I believe that the plan, purpose, and promise of God is predicated on the person or people you are willing to leave behind that prohibit your purpose. Your life is ready to experience the greatness of God when you are ready to give up who, and what, you deem as great for your life. Could it be that some things won't happen for your life until certain people are no longer close in your life?

If your life is going to another level, you have to know that everything and everyone can't go with you. You can't get to what's right for your life if you're too busy, bogged down, and burdened by the wrong things, and until you identify the bad weight that is keeping you from moving forward. When it comes to relationship wellness, you must ask, what's the reason for this relationship? Sometimes a shared experience does become a starting point for a relationship, but great relationships need to be built on much more than commonalities.

Abraham and Lot had both shared pain and a shared past. The two men bonded through a shared loss. In their case, it was the death of Abraham's brother, Lot's father, Haran (Gen. 11). Abraham's father, Terah, stopped and settled in the place where Abraham's brother died, which shows us that his father allowed the pain of loss to paralyze him because he could not move beyond the place of his pain. When you have a shared past and shared pain, it's very difficult to shift away from the relationship with those you have these shared experiences with.

While similar experiences may serve as a bond between two people in a healthy relationship, shared pain or a shared past is not a good reason to develop a deeper relationship with someone. If your relationship is built on a shared past or shared pain as the foundation, it may be toxic. It's time to take an honest look at the relationship and make sure it is based on more than common history or hurt. Otherwise, that person or people may become to you what Lot was to Abraham: a big problem. Is the relationship healthy?

Scripture never records that Lot made a single positive contribution to the trip toward Canaan or to Abraham's life. He was nothing but trouble and added no value to Abraham. He simply drained his uncle's time, resources, and energy. The blessing and prosperity that Lot experienced was a direct result from his connection to Abraham, who amassed considerable wealth (Gen. 12:16; 13:2). Who are you going above and beyond for in your life that is not willing to do anything for you except continually drain you?

Does your relationship share the same values or similar convictions? There are some relationships that no matter what you do and how much you attempt to help, the relationships will not be healthy or well with you.

I have learned firsthand that certain relationships come at the cost of frustration as I believe that there are five types of people that you can't help practically outside of prayer:

1. Those who don't know they need help.
2. Those who know they need help and don't want it.
3. Those who know they need help and don't want it from you.
4. Those who want help, but they aren't ready for it.
5. Those who want help but want it their way.

He concluded that the only way to help certain people is to intercede in prayer on their behalf. I have come to learn that some people have gimmick relationships. As long as you are buying, they will keep hanging. As long as you keep treating, they will keep eating. In a relationship, your frustration is always an indication that what you are doing isn't working. Is the relationship healthy?

A final aspect of assessing relationship health is to have a relationship not based or built on secrets or undisclosed information.

Most of us are familiar with the saying, "What you don't know won't hurt you." The problem with that assertion is that it's wrong, because what we don't know can hurt us; it can destroy us and devastate our relationships and cancel out our connections. People are destroyed for a lack of knowledge (Hosea 4:6). In the area of relationships and connections, there is a law against the things we don't know that can potentially become a problem prohibiting our purposes and creating dilemmas that delay our destinies. Is your relationship unhealthy because it is a secret?

Secrets build invisible walls around us; walls that other people perceive but cannot penetrate. What we don't know also prevents transparency, openness, and intimacy because it forces us to tiptoe around certain subjects. It will keep us from giving all of ourselves to another person and from fully receiving all the good others offer us. Keeping secrets will exhaust us, perhaps frighten us, and ultimately separate us from people we love and people who love us. "For who knows a person's thoughts except their own spirit within them?" (1 Cor. 2:11 NIV).

While you cannot take responsibility for finding out the secrets of others, you can make sure that secrets do not hide inside you. One of the best ways to position yourself to be a strong, healthy contributor to every relational connection is to make sure that you live "in the light," free from the bondage and destructive influence of secrets. "But if we walk in the light, as he is in the light, we have fellowship with one another, and the blood of Jesus, his Son, purifies us from all sin" (1 John 1:7, NIV).

When you live in the light, you will see what's right. One of the biggest barriers to intimacy and one of the most destructive forces in relationships is a secret. My assignment is to give you an opportunity to deal with the intimacy barrier in yourself that contributes to broken relationships, so that you can be a healthy, strong participator in the purpose that comes from great relationships.

Before your relationship can shift to where it needs to be, you must be aware of where the relationship health is right now regarding any secrets. Ask yourself these questions:

What is it about my thoughts, words, or actions that I do not want other people to know?

What am I most ashamed of about my past or about my life today?

What am I most afraid to share with my spouse, potential spouse, or closest friends?

Maybe you don't have any deep, dark secrets. If you do, this assessment can provide awareness that can be the catalyst to bringing change to your life and empower you to enjoy a quality of relationship with others you have never known before. The enemy uses secrets to steal away the blessings of the relationship and to sever the connection, because the right people are connected to your destiny.

The interactions of Samson and Delilah in their relationship are proof that secrets can destroy both individuals and the relationships those individuals have with others. Delilah's secret motive for the relationship became the tool that the enemy used to seduce Samson out of the place of God's purpose. The strength of Samson's life was a secret that could only be trusted by the right person or the right people. Who are you trusting with the secrets of your life that you shouldn't be? Do you know the motive of your relationship connections?

Secrets are always linked to the source of something else beneath the surface. The damaging effect of secrets in Samson's relationships didn't start with Delilah and his hair. Samson had a pattern of establishing relationships that were not based on truth or authenticity. The evidence of this destructive pattern begins in Judges 14. Going to Timnah put Samson on a precarious path, as it led him to the place (vineyards) that was prohibited by his purpose. This was because he would be faced with a temptation to do something that he shouldn't have been faced with if he wasn't in this place. As a Nazarite, Samson was instructed by God to stay away from (seed to skin) wine, vinegar, grape juice, fresh grape, and raisins (Num. 6:3-4).

The wrong things will catch you off guard when your life is not in the place it should be. Although God's action of divine intervention and empowerment spared Samson's life, it didn't keep Samson's problems from being multiplied. When he killed the lion, he broke a second part of his Nazarite vow, touching a dead body (Num. 6:6). He must have suffered silently, because Judges 14:6 informs us that he did not tell his parents about the lion; he kept the matter a secret.

Secret places lead to secret battles. When you go to places with people who you know you don't belong with, it will result in battles that could have been avoided. When people take the risk of going to places they shouldn't go, trouble is always at hand because a battle is guaranteed to break out. These places could be physical places that could cause physical harm or emotional turmoil to the soul, such as jealousy, anger, or bitterness, that could harm your heart or drive you to "cyber" places, such as pornographic websites, that could destroy your mind, or lead you to places of bad habits or bad influences. Don't get to a place where you take for granted the privilege of the relationship and assume that you can do anything you want and keep the benefits that come as a result of the relationship. Every relationship moves at the speed of trust. Love is required, but trust is earned.

Don't hesitate to put someone on trial before moving to a deeper level of relationship and connection. Go ahead and ask personal questions; your life demands it and your purpose requires it. Initiate discussions about attitudes or behaviors that concern you. When you suspect a secret, trust your instincts and intuition. People with serious secrets may not be forthcoming with answers but take notice of the way they handle the question. Does it seem to make them nervous? Does their body language change? Do they immediately switch to another topic of conversation? Do they laugh at you or become defensive? These types of responses may indicate that something negative or potentially damaging lurks beneath the surface and needs to be investigated more fully.

Answers to questions result in awareness; awareness produces accountability for purpose and progressively grows the relationship connection in a healthy way that functions properly for the benefit of those in the relationship. Though we do need to make some effort to find out whether the people we are in relationships with have things hidden under the visible level of their lives, we are limited in our abilities to unearth other people's secrets. We do, however, have complete control over our own lives and the way we handle things we choose to do.

We can create or keep our personal secrets, or we can live openly and transparently with our trusted friends and colleagues. We can set ourselves up for disappointment and harm, which may impact people we care about, or we can position ourselves for great relationships by being honest about our temptations and failings instead of excusing or hiding them. Is your relationship a secret?

CHAPTER 6

IT's the Law!

What is governing your relationship? How do you protect your relationship? If your relationships are not protected by boundaries, your life can veer off course and become a wreck. The relationship law of boundaries is for your protection. Does your relationship have boundaries? The laws of your relationship that are implemented by you, will help you, and not hurt you. A failure to adhere to the laws for relationship will hinder your ability to set up boundaries for your life that should bless you and not stress you. What does law mean?

I believe that law is essentially a rule to define a certain behavior to govern something. Our world is set up with laws and principles. In like manner and in the context of relationship, when laws are broken and principles are violated in relationship, consequences of delays happen in your life. For your relationship to move in the right direction, you need to know the laws of boundaries and share those laws with those you are in relationship with. Relational boundaries are for everyone's benefit. I believe that every relationship must have established boundaries to grow healthy or the relationship will be violated.

In this chapter, I want to look at some relationship laws that should be used to govern your relationships.

There are five laws for relationships that can be used for your protection:

1. The law of sowing and reaping
2. The law of responsibility
3. The law of power
4. The law of respect
5. The law of motivation

Law #1–The law of sowing and reaping: This law of cause and effect is a basic law of life. Scripture teaches us that we will get whatever we give (Gal. 6:7 NIV). This law is not punishment, it is the reality of our protection. If you don't reap what you sow, it's only because someone else stepped in and reaped the consequences for you.

Are you in a relationship that allows you to interrupt this law by stepping in and rescuing an irresponsible person? Rescuing a person from the natural consequences of his/her behavior enables the person to continue in irresponsible behavior. A person who continually rescues another person is a codependent. In effect, codependent, boundary-less people cosign the note of life for the irresponsible person. When you establish boundaries, it helps codependent people to stop interrupting the law of sowing and reaping in their loved ones' lives. When this has continued to happen in your relationship, it's time to confront the person that you desire to see change. Confronting an irresponsible person is not painful to the person, but the results are from his/her decisions.

Blessings continually given prematurely will always stunt the growth and development of an irresponsible person. As believers, we can't break spiritual laws and violate God's principles without dealing with some type of consequences.

Law #2–The law of responsibility: The law of responsibility includes loving others. The commandment to love is the entire law for Christians (John 13:34-35 NIV). Anytime you are not loving others, you aren't taking full responsibility for yourself; you have disowned your heart. Problems arise when boundaries of responsibility are confused. We are to love one another, not be one another. I can't feel your feelings for you. I can't think for you. I can't behave for you. I can't work through disappointment that limits bring for you. In short, I can't grow for you; only you can. Likewise, you can't grow for me.

You are responsible for yourself, and I am responsible for myself. The law of responsibility also applies to our responsibility to treat others the way we would want to be treated. If we were down and out, helpless and without hope, we would certainly want help and provision; this is the other side of being responsible "to."

This aspect of being responsible "to" is not only in the giving but in the setting of limits on another's destructive and irresponsible behavior. It is not good to rescue someone from the consequences of his/her sin, for you will only have to do it again. You have reinforced the pattern (Prov. 19:19). It is the same principle spoken of in child-rearing; it is hurtful to not have limits with others, because it leads them to destruction (Prov. 23:13).

Law #3 – The law of power: The law of power is not powerlessness. John the Evangelist says that we are all in that state and that anyone who denies it is lying (1 John 1:8).

Though you do not have the power in and of yourself to overcome these patterns, you do have the power to do some things that will bring fruits of victory later:

1. You have the power to agree with the truth about your problems. (The Bible calls this a "confession.") To confess means to "agree with." You have the ability to at least say, "That is me." You may not be able to change it yet, but you can confess.

2. You have the power to submit your inability to God. (You always have the power to ask for help and yield. You have the power to humble yourself and turn your life over to Him. You may not be able to make yourself well, but you

can contact a doctor. The humbling of yourself commanded in the Bible is always coupled with great promises. If you do what you are able—confess, believe, and ask for help—God will do what you are unable to do—bring about change (1 John 1:9, James 4:7-10, Matt. 5:3, 6)).

3. You have the power to turn from the evil that you find within you. (This is called repentance. This doesn't mean that you'll be perfect; it means that you can see your sinful parts as aspects that you want to change.)

4. You have the power to humble yourself and ask God and others to help you with your developmental injuries and leftover childhood needs. (Many of our problematic parts come from being empty inside, and you need to seek God and others to have those needs met.)

5. You have the power to seek out those you have injured and make amends. (You need to do this in order to be responsible for yourself and your behavior (sin) and be responsible to those you have injured. Matthew 5:23-24 says, "Therefore, if you are offering your gift at the altar and there remember that your brother has something against you, leave your gift there in front of the altar. First go and be reconciled to your brother; then come and offer your gift.")

These are boundaries that help define what you do not have power over; everything outside of them.

Law #4 – The law of respect: In most relationships, one word continues to come up again and again when people describe their problems with setting boundaries: *they*. "But *they* accept me if I say no. They will get angry if I set limits and do this. But they won't speak to me for a week if I tell them how I really feel."

We fear that others will not respect our boundaries. We focus on others and lose clarity about ourselves. Sometimes, the problem is that we judge others' boundaries by saying or thinking things such as this: "How could he refuse to come by and pick me up? It's right on his way! He could find some 'time alone' some other time." "That's so selfish of her to not come to the luncheon. After all, the rest of us are sacrificing." "What do you mean, no? I just need the money for a little while. It seems that, after all I do for you, you could at least do me this one little favor."

In the relationship vehicle of life, you must understand that everyone doesn't drive like you. Everyone doesn't have the same boundaries as you or live with the same expectations as you. We judge the boundary decisions of others, thinking that we know best how they "ought" to give and usually that means "they ought to give to me the way I want them to."

When we judge others' boundaries, ours will fall under the same judgment. If we condemn others' boundaries, we expect them to condemn ours. This sets up the fear cycle inside that makes us afraid to set boundaries that we need to set. As a result, we comply, then we resent, and the "love" that we have given goes sour. This is where the law of respect occurs. As Jesus said, "So in everything, do to others what you would have them do to you" (Matt. 7:12 NIV).

We need to respect the boundaries of others. We need to love the boundaries of others in order to command respect for our own. You will always get what you give. You give attitude all of the time? You will get an attitude that discourages people from wanting to be around you in return. Is there respect in the relationship? We need to treat the boundaries of others the way we want them to treat ours. If we love and respect people who tell us no, they will love and respect our no. Freedom is found in the relationship when someone exercises his/her ability to say no.

Your real concern with others should not be "Are they doing what I would do or what I want them to do?" but "Are they really making a free choice?" When we accept others' freedom, we don't get angry, feel guilty, or withdraw our love when they set boundaries with us. When we accept others' freedom, we feel better about our own.

Law #5 – The law of motivation: Some people are confused and have misinterpreted the true understanding that it is more blessed to give than to receive, and their lives are living with false understanding. Are you frequently feeling unappreciated for all that you are doing for other people and wishing that they would have more consideration for your time and energy? Feeling like whenever someone wanted something from you, you just do it? You do this because you think that this is loving and you want to be a loving person, right? These feelings not submitted to healthy boundaries and established laws of life for your relationship will cause fatigue to grow into depression, because you feel as though you are loving too much when actually you don't love yourself.

True love leads to a blessed state and a state of cheer. Love brings fulfillment and joy in the soul, not depression. If your love is depressing you, it's not love; it's a yoke and a bondage that you need to quit carrying.

What's the motivation and reason behind what you do? What's your why in the relationship? Are you doing and sacrificing in fear? Doing things for people out of fear is rooted in a past experience where love was withdrawn from you when you didn't do what someone wanted. This results in you learning the behavior to give reluctantly. The motive for giving isn't love, but fear of losing love and being afraid of other people's anger if you had a past experience of being yelled at for not doing what someone wanted you to do. This caused a learned behavior of fearing angry confrontations and saying no to others. Remember, self-centered people often get angry when someone tells them no.

Saying yes out of fear that you will lose love and that other people will be angry at you are false motives and hinders you from setting boundaries. What's the motive in your relationship?

1. Fear of loss of love or abandonment: People who say yes and then resent saying yes in fear of losing someone's love. Don't give to get love; otherwise, when you don't get it, you will feel abandoned.
2. Fear of others' anger: Because of old hurts and poor boundaries, some people can't stand for anyone to be mad at them.
3. Fear of loneliness: Some people give in to others because they feel that will win love and end loneliness.
4. Fear of losing the "good me" inside: We are made to love and as a result, when we are not loving, we are in pain. Many people cannot say, "I love you, and I do not want to do that." They think that to love means to always say yes.
5. Guilt: Many people's giving is motivated by guilt. They are trying to do enough good things to overcome the guilt inside and feel good about themselves. When they say no, they feel bad. So they keep trying to earn a sense of goodness.
6. Payback: Many people have received things with guilt messages attached. For example, someone may say things like, "I never had it as good as you. You should be ashamed at all you get." They feel a burden to pay for all they have been given.
7. Approval: Many feel as if they are still children seeking parental approval. When someone wants something from them, they need to give so that this symbolic parent will be well pleased.
8. Over-identification with the others' loss: Many times, people have not dealt with all of their own disappointments and losses, so whenever they deny someone else with a no, they feel the other person's sadness to highest degree. They can't stand to hurt someone that badly, so they comply.

The point is that we were called into freedom, and this freedom results in gratitude, an overflowing heart and love for others. To give bountifully has great rewards; it is truly more blessed to give than to receive. If your giving is not leading to cheer, then you need to examine the Law of Motivation, which says this: Freedom first, service second. If you serve to get free of your fear, you are doomed to failure. Let God work on the fears, resolve them, and create some healthy boundaries to guard the freedom you were called to have.

Living with the wrong motives in your relationship will cause you to do foolish things that negate the wisdom you need to prosper in your life. "Beloved, I pray that you may prosper in all things and be in health, just as your soul prospers" (3 John 1:2, NKJV).

Relational wellness is essential to your life. If you are dealing with a person or people you know is not right for you, but you keep them around anyway, the problem is that the longer you keep them around, the more they will take a toll on you mentally, emotionally, and spiritually. This will lead you to a point where you cannot move forward with the right person or people, because you will still experience damage and will have to heal from the person or people who were never the right fit for your life. Don't allow people to make you feel guilty for wanting to move on; if they would have valued your life, then moving on would have never been an option.

I am praying that you will no longer suffer relationship sickness because of your failed efforts to change someone who doesn't want to change. You are empowered to enforce these laws and principles in your life. Your peace is sometimes connected to the separation from some people's presence in your life.

Be assured and encouraged that you are not alone and God already knows what He is going to do. I'm praying that the Holy Spirit will lead the right people to you, while also leading you to the right people. I pray for divine connections and that every relationship with evil intent to harm you would be diminished. I pray that the truth becomes evident and that freedom becomes inevitable. You are attracting wise, loving, and compassionate people in your life space who possess the skills and resources to help you move on to the next place in your life. You're being divinely connected to everything and everybody that you need to overcome your past, what you did, and what you have been through. You are receiving reciprocal relationships into your life and connecting to people who value and respect who you are and what's on your life. Choose to embrace them, and even if you were once intimidated by them and afraid that you wouldn't fit into their circle of friends and influence, say yes to what's next and amen to what has been spoken over your life. You're connected, covered, converted, changed, cared for, and courageous. Your next move will be the best move, for you're shifting in your relationship.

My prayer is that you will clarify your boundaries in your relationship and alleviate the stress in your soul. You can work on submitting yourself to the process and working with God to change you. You cannot change anything else: not the weather, the past, the economy, and especially not other people. You cannot change others. More people suffer from trying to change others than from any other sickness. It is impossible.

What you can do is influence others, and there is a way. Since you cannot get them to change, you must change yourself so that their destructive patterns no longer work on you. Change your way of dealing with them; they may be motivated to change if their old ways no longer work. When it comes to your RelationShift, you must know that it's the law for you to have boundaries for your life.

If this area is a struggle or strain for you to practically apply in the area of your relationships, make this declaration: Boundaries are always for my protection and benefit. I am empowered from this point in my life forward to take responsibility for and ownership of my life by knowing when to say yes, how to say no, and take control of my life. I am benefitting from the assurance that gives me a hope that I can thrive instead of just survive. How will you govern your relationship?

CHAPTER 7

Where Is IT Going?

The quality of your life is interlinked, intertwined, and interconnected to the relationships in your life. The greatest benefit people can have is their connection to the right people that are in their lives, whereas the biggest hindrance to people is often tied to the wrong associations in their lives. Relationships (connections) are destiny determinants or purpose prohibitors. RelationShift in this chapter is about your relationship movement.

As a disclaimer, let me share with you some insight I've learned in life: Everybody can't go everywhere with you because the vehicle to your destiny always has limited seating. Everybody kissing you aren't clinging to you because everybody that loves you (and whom you love) can't go with you. Some of your problems exist to reveal the motives and places that people hold in your life. Everybody that leaves you doesn't hate you, because not everyone who chooses not to go with you is being disloyal. Some people love you enough to know that they can't go with you to the next place.

Don't become angry, because people know where their stop is in your life. Let people love you from where they are and bind up the enemy that tries to tell you that you're being rejected. They didn't turn away and turn around because they're rejecting you or where you're going; they just accepted the truth in their own lives and they recognize that they can't go with you.

Could it be that some of the reason for you waiting on what you have been praying for is based on the fact that sometimes God gives you the time to shift from some people who no longer fit the timing of the season that your life is in currently? Every new season demands a circumcised circle. Cut all the iffy and sketchy people off before you soon find out that they may be prohibiting your purpose and distracting you away from your destiny. As we explore your relationship movement further, ask yourself these questions:

1. Do you know where your relationships are going?
2. Are you aware of the place you're in with people?
3. Are you clear on what season and stage you're in with the close connections in your life?

If you are not clear on where your relationships are going, how do you know if the relationship is a part of God's plan for your life? Nothing will test, try, and train your circle of connections more than transition. You will always have a crowd of people clamoring for your attention pre-test, but God uses the shift, movement, and transition for change to expose the heart of a person, people, and circle in your life.

My prayer for you, as you're reading this book, is that God gives you a greater sense of understanding, knowledge, and revelation of who's who in your life. The awareness of the place you stand with a person or people will be the key that accelerates your life forward faster or slows you down and further delays where you're headed on your journey of life.

In 2 Kings 2, Elijah and Elisha take a final journey (the season right before permanent change happens, the stage that sets you up for success and the step that accelerates your life beyond your present situations) together before Elijah goes to heaven (next level, highest place, promotion of earthly life). Each place they go in 2 Kings 2 is highly symbolic, representing a necessary and vital aspect of all healthy and right relationships.

If you want your relationships to be healthy, function right, and become mature, you can also expect to go through the situations these places represent. I would go as far as to say that if a relationship is going to be strong and healthy, it must follow the same course, metaphorically, that Elijah and Elisha traveled.

If we were to track their relationship journey on a map, we would see that they travel together to four places in 2 Kings 2: Gilgal (v. 1), Bethel (v. 2), Jericho (v. 4), and the Jordan River (v. 6-8). These places are familiar to most Bible readers because of their historical significance, but they also represent significant experiences in our relationships.

When Joshua led the Israelites into the Promised Land years before Elijah lived, the first place they came to after crossing the Jordan River was Gilgal (Josh. 5:1-9). This was the location where Joshua observed the covenant ritual of circumcision for the Hebrew males who were not circumcised, prior to entering the Promised Land, so Gilgal is a place that symbolizes the cutting of the flesh.

In every thriving relationship, the blade of truth and honesty must be applied at times. If two people cannot have honest communication that sometimes hurts, the relationship will be superficial at best. We have heard that "the truth hurts," and sometimes it does. When the truth is delivered with love, even painful honesty leads to relational health and strength. This is true for romantic and platonic relationships, and it is also true in the workplace and in families, churches, and social organizations.

Throughout Scripture, Bethel is known as a place of prayer and worship. Any healthy connection will stretch you and push you to prayer and worship through its challenges and its joys. I believe that any believer who is part of a strong, healthy marriage would admit to going through some difficult situations in which one or the other, or both spouses, had to take the circumstances to God in prayer. There are times in such an intimate relationship that two people need divine help and intervention, and the only way to ask for it is through prayer. There are also times when the relationship is strong and blissful, and the only way to respond is to thank and worship God. If you are a believer, you can pray and worship your way through and know that some situations will call for fervent prayer to see you through beyond where you are.

The city of Jericho has long been known as a fortified city of thick walls and strongholds, which symbolize the walls we erect around ourselves. Are you building walls to keep others from getting too close or to keep from giving too much of yourself to others in relationships?

Sometimes knowing others deeply and allowing ourselves to be deeply known can cause us to feel vulnerable, which results in us feeling more secure if we refuse to let it happen. A thriving relationship is only possible with a person who will not allow you to hide behind those walls or remain entrenched in strongholds.

The sea into which the Jordan River flows is called "dead" because it does not give, preserve, or sustain life. Nothing lives in the Dead Sea; plant and sea life that flow into it die quickly. Symbolically, the last place Elijah and Elisha visit together speaks to death. One of the most foundational truths of thriving relationships is that they are impossible unless both parties involved are willing to die to themselves. They must be willing to lay aside their rights, agendas, and goals, doing what Romans 12:10 says to do: "Be devoted to one another in love. Honor one another above yourselves."

If you've ever been a part of a relationship in which both people die to themselves, you know that the most amazing thing happens as a result: Two individuals willingly put to death their personal preferences and aspirations, and a great relationship comes to life. In a world that seems to be spinning faster and faster, certain things still just take time and require a necessary process.

You cannot rush the gestation period of a human being; we cannot push the earth to rotate on its axis any more rapidly; and we cannot speed up the passage of time. Likewise, no one can successfully rush the development of a thriving relationship; it takes hours, days, weeks, months, and years. Healthy relationships take time to build, because they must undergo certain situations and be tested in the crucible of circumstances. Relationships are forged in all sorts of ways, and while the specifics may vary, the need for the process remains constant. Strong relationships are worth the investments of time and energy they require. I encourage you to position yourself for the best relationships you have ever known by understanding the process they must go through and devoting yourself to it. Where is your relationship going?

CHAPTER 8

IT's Time to Accelerate!

Every relationship moves at the speed of trust. A relationship that is not tested is a relationship that can't be trusted. Relationships are the vehicle in your life and will help you move forward or prevent you from moving into God's purpose. The right relationships will push you in the right direction, while the wrong relationships will hold you back by forcing your life into overdrive mode and wear down the tread of your life. If your circle causes you to run around in circles, it's time to get a new circle before you wear yourself down and miss out on what God has already purposed and promised you. All delays are not divine. Some things aren't happening because of the relationships you're still trying to carry and move with.

Since the beginning of time, when God wanted to accomplish something, He consistently used two critical components: God's word and a person. If you take a close look at Scripture, you will clearly see that everything God has done from creation onward, He has done through His Word and a human being.

This theme is found in some of the significant works of God throughout history:

1. Preserving humanity and animals in the flood through Noah.
2. The birth and growth of God's people from Egyptian slavery through Moses.
3. Leading His people into the Promised Land through Joshua.

4. The rebuilding of the walls around Jerusalem through Nehemiah.
5. Bringing salvation to the Gentiles through the apostle Paul.
6. Redeeming humanity through Jesus Christ.

The principle of partnership between God's Word and a person is well established. Whenever God wants to bless one person's life (including yours), He will do it through His Word and a person. God will intentionally place people in your life for the sole reason of blessing you and elevating your quality of life, just as He has done for generations. For the Bible readers and learners of God's Word, think about it: Jacob was blessed because of Isaac, Joseph was blessed because of Pharaoh, Joshua was blessed because of Moses, Samuel was blessed because of Eli, and David was blessed because of Jonathan.

Here is a question we must consider: Who is being blessed because of you?

The principle is that in order for people both in biblical times and today to enjoy thriving (healthy and growing) relationships, certain characteristics and attitudes must be present and a process must be allowed to unfold. For your relationship to accelerate and advance further, it requires three things:

1. Endurance
2. Engagement
3. Example

When endurance, engagement, and examples exist in any relationship, that connection can advance at a faster pace and be more flexible as it grows and develops over time. Is your relationship in a position to accelerate?

Another aspect and attribute that will assist any relationship in the advancement of its development is a relationship that is a wise connection. The truth is that relationships are destiny determinants. They either assist or inhibit, help or hinder, bless or stress, build or destroy, add or take away, as you journey to God's best. His principles are the blueprint that will lead you to fruitful, flourishing, and fulfilling relationships.

Whoever has your ear automatically gets your life. The voice that constantly speaks into you is the determining factor that will always influence you. Out of season people who you give your ear to end up with a hold on your life that keeps you stuck in the past. Proverbs 13:20 (NIV), "Walk with the wise and become wise, for a companion of fools suffers harm."

The times we are living in require you to guard your ear as much as you try to guard your heart. If the wrong person gets your ear, the heart will follow suit, and the wrong person will have a hold on your life. If a man's opinion has a hold on your life, your destiny is deterred and misguided in the wrong direction. You must learn to quit listening to just anybody. You can't afford to buy the counsel, advice, direction, feedback, and comments from someone who doesn't add value and substance to your life from what he/she is telling you. Are you using relationship wisdom?

Relationship wisdom is the key to accelerating your relationship with others. How can you know if the relationship you have with someone is a wise choice for your life? Pay attention to their lives and believe what you see before you focus on what you hear. If their lives are Spirit-led in an area that you need counsel or direction in, you will see the fruit that will bear witness to that area in their lives.

Quit talking and asking down and start talking and asking up. A single person who has never been married is not in a position to truly give a married couple marital advice or counsel. A person who has always lived at someone else's home and never had to pay bills on his/her own shouldn't be talking to you about managing responsibility or budgeting and balancing your checkbook. You can't impart what you haven't received or walked out in your own life. Whatever counsel from whoever you're listening to will lead you in one direction or another.

Scripture provides us with an example of a relationship that wasn't based on wisdom and caused a delay in the destiny of a man because the relationship wasn't credible. Ahithophel was a cherished and esteemed companion of David. They enjoyed a close friendship, not unlike that between David and Jonathan. Psalm 55:12-14 references this relationship: "A man mine equal, my guide, and mine acquaintance. We took sweet council together and walked unto the house of God in company." David depended upon Ahithophel's wise counsel (2 Sam. 16:23).

It had been the long desire of Absalom to replace his father David on the throne of Israel (2 Sam. 15). He harbored anger in his heart that turned to bitterness and hatred against his father, after his sister Tamar was raped by their half-brother Amnon. David was angry but failed to deal with the matter. After two years, Absalom took matters into his own hands and murdered Amnon at Baal-hazor (2 Sam. 13:28-29). Absalom fled to Geshur (home of his mother's family) where he remained for three years. David was tricked into receiving him back, but it was another two years before he would meet with Absalom (2 Sam. 14).

Absalom summoned Ahithophel to him from Giloh, and from 2 Samuel 15:12, we learn that Ahithophel gave support to the cause of Absalom. Ahithophel advised the immediate pursuit of David, which may well have resulted in David's defeat, but Absalom followed the counsel of Hushai the Archite (left by David as his spy in Jerusalem) and waited. Ahithophel was aware of the impending disaster and we read in 2 Samuel 17:23 NIV, "When Ahithophel saw that his advice had not been followed, he saddled his donkey and set out for his house in his hometown. He put his house in order and then hanged himself..."

We would do well to be guided by the scriptural record of Ahithophel and remember that our relationships and associations will influence us to go in one direction or another and to avoid foolishness at all costs, because wisdom is the principal thing. Whatever you get (counsel, feedback, and advice) from people around you, make sure you gain an understanding (Prov. 4:7).

CHAPTER 9

Is IT a Distraction?

What is stopping or blocking you from what you need to be focused on in your life? Imagine the difficulty of safe driving when you become distracted. Accidents become more likely when there is driver inattention. When understanding this occurrence, we can agree that distracted driving is any activity that could divert a person's attention away from the primary task of driving. I believe that all distractions endanger driver, passenger, and bystander safety.

On the road of life, you can't go where you desire to be, if your relationship is a distraction to where you are going. A failure to address distracting activity can result in relationship accidents that could have been prevented. We must ask ourselves this question: Is the relationship a distraction to my life's focus?

As long as you are only doing what someone else wants you to do, your life will be limited to only what he/she wants for you. People don't have a problem with the truth of who you are until it is no longer a convenience for them. If you only do what they want you to do, you nullify the purpose of God for your life. The central issue of any relationship shows up the moment you begin to do what God has purposed for you to do. People accept the truth of who you are until your life begins to implement that truth for your life. When you have an authentic relationship established on the covenant principles of God, He will give someone insight into who you really are, and it is at that moment that what God said will be accepted or resisted. If your life is being and doing what God said, don't allow someone else's resistance to divert your attention away from what God said concerning you.

A failure to deal with distractions in your relationship can lead to an extreme agitation of the mind, which plays on your emotions. You don't have the time to be stuck in your feelings in this season. You have somewhere to go, somewhere to be, and something to do, because other lives are waiting on you to get there. If your advice is based on your opinion, keep it to yourself so that you aren't a distraction. You should be quick to disallow anything that tries to distract you. When our focus is of the same thing, we can drive together without being distracted by activity that can lead to accidents.

Living and learning through people in my life has taught me that there are three levels of healthy relationships that are needed to help you fulfill your purpose in life. I believe that these levels are corporate, casual, and close relationship connections. Your ability to manage and discern your relationships is vitally important and highly essential to your overall well-being, and the difference in you being able to focus on what you're assigned to, and responsible for, doing in your life.

It is essential to build relationships and to understand how to navigate and successfully manage them during every season of life. This is true for every type of human relationship possible—at every age, in professional, social, and familial settings. It is also important to discern who people are in your life and which dimension of relationship to place them in accordingly.

We must choose to delve deeper in our relationships and connections to reach the three-dimensions. It doesn't happen haphazardly or coincidently: God presents opportunities through people in front of you, but you must be willing to do the work through prayer, observation, and experience to discern which dimension each relationship you have should be strategically placed.

While this concept may sound rigid to some in discussing human relationships, applying this system will provide the necessary discipline and establish the right boundaries to guard our hearts and pursue what God has called us to do effectively, with minimal distractions.

The first principle that will help you realize the right relationships and connections for your life should be based on the mindset that when it comes to the right people in your life on purpose, you should shift from quantity to quality. More is not always a guarantee for better. As your circle gets smaller, your vision will grow wider. You will see God move and do more in your life when some people leave. The greatest growth seems to take place when there is some form of absence.

You must place a premium on discerning relationships effectively, which allows you to look at the hearts of people before deeply connecting to them. It also helps you to honor the real and authentic connections in your life. The longer you live, the more you will realize the importance and essentialism of having the right people in your life. An "old way of thinking" that you must RelationShift from is assuming that having more connections and more people around you will equate to more success. Quality is always greater than quantity.

Are you ready to take a glance and get a glimpse of this principle at work?

Matthew 9:23-26 (NIV) says:

> When Jesus entered the synagogue leader's house and saw the noisy crowd and people playing pipes, he said, "Go away. The girl is not dead but asleep." But they laughed at him. After the crowd had been put outside, he went in and took the girl by the hand, and she got up. News of this spread through all that region.

In this narrative, Jesus went to Jairus's home to heal his daughter, who was pronounced dead on arrival. This text teaches us the importance of discerning relationships because of Jesus's behavior. Despite the notion that all these individuals were in Jairus's home prior to Jesus's arrival, Jesus immediately recognized and discerned the personal nature of the miracle that He was going to perform. Jesus kicked all the unnecessary people out of that intimate space. Specifically, Jesus put the professional mourners out, who said, "She's not sleep; she's dead." This notion is powerful and one that we should adopt in our lives: An important part of discerning relationships is identifying when we have come to a point when it is necessary (for our own well-being and growth) to put certain people out of our lives or out of our private and personal space.

To see what seems impossible happen in your life, you must have relationships around you to believe that anything is possible for you, and not be distractions trying to deter your focus and hinder you. Situations, circumstances, and conditions are the catalysts that the Lord uses to cause you to recognize on purpose and realize who's who in your life that helps you to fulfill what is destined. Real eyes realize real lies. Discern who's who in your life. You don't need the feelings and opinions of everyone; you just need the faith of the right ones.

When you shift and separate yourself from the uninspired, unexcited, unbelieving, and the ungrateful, get ready to witness the working of His wonders in the area of the uncommon. We cannot expect a miracle until the room (area, place, and space) of our lives are clear of doubters and mockers containing only those who walk close enough with us to believe for us, through the difficult and the seemingly impossible, to see change happen and becomes visible. Is your relationship a faith distraction?

CHAPTER 10

Is IT Time to Go?

Where God calls your life to be, you're purposed to go, but as you grow, you need to know that everyone can't go everywhere with you. When it's time to shift the relationship and go, is it going forward with you becomes the question for your soul.

Being that purpose represents a place; where God guides you in the vehicle of your life on your journey to destiny, your life will have limited seating. The only room you have is to accommodate those who are willing to grow and go with you. The quality of your life is interlinked, intertwined, and interconnected to the relationships in your life. The greatest source of blessing is connected to the right people who God has placed in your life, and the biggest hindrance to your purpose is often tied to the wrong associations in your life.

Since relationships (connections) are destiny determinants or purpose prohibitors, you need to clearly know when and how to end an unhealthy relationship. Unhealthy connections are not profitable for your soul. "Do two walk together unless they have agreed to do so?" (Amos 3:3 NIV).

The right relationships in your life are not about an agreement on preferences: it's about the agreement on God's plan, purpose, and promise concerning those in the relationship. To live your life directed by destiny will demand you make difficult decisions and choices that bring change to your life on purpose. Do you know when and how to end an unhealthy relationship?

The most difficult choices in relationships often involve whether or not to remain in someone's life or to allow someone to remain in yours, when problems arise. In Christian circles, we frequently take a naive approach to relationships, urging people to love one another, as Scripture admonishes, while failing to understand and acknowledge how complicated loving others can become.

If we believe God leads us into relationships with people, we also tend to think those relationships must last for the rest of our lives. To the best of my knowledge, the only interpersonal relationship bound by solemn vows and the promise "until death do us part" is the covenant of marriage. In other types of relationships, we may find that we have lifelong friends, or we may discover that certain people are part of our lives for a specific purpose during a certain period of time. We may also end up in relationships we wish would last for years but that end prematurely for various reasons.

My prayer and aim through this chapter are to help you clearly understand and see some of the most common and valid reasons certain relationships must come to a close, and to help you know how to bring closure in loving, gracious ways. There are relational lessons stemming from the connections of Abraham and Lot, as you've learned that helping some people simply is not worth what it costs to those who try to assist them.

Paul and John Mark's RelationShift demonstrates what happens when a relationship starts out well and is filled with promise, but one person gets upset and chooses to leave. Scripturally, we find that there are relational connections between Ruth, Orpah, and Naomi that highlight the differences between covenant partners—people who come into your life to stay loyal and committed through it all—and halfway friends—people with whom you have relationships for a specific reason or for an appointed season.

As we delve deeper into His Word to connect His truth to the areas that affect our relationships, I pray that you will have as many relationships that help you, not hinder you, as possible. When you find yourself in a place where you must shift from people and bring the relationship to an end, I hope you will remember these principles and be empowered to do it well in your walk with others. Regardless of the many reasons for a separation, we sometimes need to ask or allow someone who has been a valuable or even vital part of our lives to leave the relationship because a once positive association has become negative. What do you do when a right relationship goes wrong?

Centuries ago, a man found himself in a situation in which a good relationship went bad and did not last. The entire story is found in the book of Acts, but I'll summarize it here. A vicious persecutor of Christians, named Saul, had an amazing encounter with God that blinded him for several days and changed his life forever. He converted from a religious Pharisee to a "souled"-out relationship with Jesus Christ as a follower of Him. He dedicated his life to evangelism, starting churches, and helping individuals and groups of believers follow Christ with ever-increasing passion and maturity.

Because of Saul's past, many Christians were skeptical and self-justified in being judgmental of him after his conversion, perhaps wondering whether or not it was genuine. Who around you that knows about your past and questions your heart for God? A man named Barnabas took Saul under his wing and helped him get started in what became a powerful, world-changing ministry. Barnabas's name actually means "encourager" or "Son of Encouragement" (Acts 4:36); and for many years he proved to be a true encourager and a supportive colleague in ministry and friendship to Saul, who later became known as the apostle Paul.

The time came when, after a season of fasting and prayer (devotion time with God), the early church in Antioch commissioned Paul and Barnabas to do the work of the ministry. They set sail for the island of Cyprus, and Barnabas's cousin, John Mark, accompanied them. Scripture specifically says John Mark went with them for the purpose of helping them. Paul and John Mark likely became acquainted through Barnabas, and the three men spent much time together. John Mark was clearly present during the early days of Paul's ministry and proved valuable enough to be invited to join Paul's first missionary journey. When Paul and Barnabas left Cyprus and traveled to Perga in the region of Pamphylia, the positive relationship between Paul and John Mark turned negative; their association ended—and it ended badly.

Do you have any relationships that will stop you from moving forward with your plans?

For years, scholars have studied and debated what caused the breach between buddies and the RelationShift between Paul and John Mark. A number of dissertations have addressed this issue, offering various theories about why they did not remain friends. No solid conclusions have been reached, but we can make two points clear with certainty.

First, John Mark was the person who left Paul and Barnabas. Apparently, he abandoned them on his volition; it was his choice, not theirs. Second, only Paul, John Mark, and perhaps Barnabas, along with a few people close to them at the time, knew exactly what happened. I certainly do not know the details of the rift, tension, or switch-up, but I am sure the dynamics they faced centuries ago were not much different from some of the circumstances you and I may face in relationships today. Newsflash! Don't become bitter because someone recognizes where his/her stop is in the journey of your life. Give the person credit that he/she was wise enough to know and clearly recognize that where you're headed, he/she wasn't fit to follow through and finish the rest of your journey with you.

Being that the separation of Paul and John Mark has sparked so much interest among Bible scholars over the years, several pre-dominant theories have emerged about why John Mark left. I want to highlight a few of them, because I believe that they hold important clues to why this relationship may have fallen apart so long ago. These theories offer important insights into how you can know if a once-good relationship in your life is beginning to turn bad and needs to move toward a close. What can we learn from the relational lessons taught by the separation of Paul and John Mark's relationship that demands and necessitates a RelationShift? What should you do when a right relationship goes wrong?

Sometimes when your purpose becomes known, it will push the buttons with some people and become the catalyst to cause the change in some of your relationships. The pursuit of your purpose is the litmus test that causes people to be drawn closer to you or the determining factor that pushes people to start drifting away from you. What you decide to do when you need to shift the relationship depends on how you see your situation with a person or people through Paul's perspective or from Barnabas's perspective. As you prayerfully consider your options, here is some practical advice on three important questions you should ask yourself when parting ways with someone who has been valuable in the past:

1. How should I think about this situation?

First, be very clear about where God is leading you and why that requires the relationship to change. This understanding will give both you and the other person a clear rationale for ending the relationship, and the boldness to do it. Second, you must understand and believe that just as God brought the person with whom you are ending a relationship into your life, God will bring others into your life as well. Be patient, prayerful, and watchful, because He will bring you the person and the people you need.

2. What do I say when I actually bring closure to the relationship?

Be sincere, because people know when someone is not being authentic. Be honest but speak with love. The need for honesty does not give you the right to trample on anyone's feelings, so choose your words wisely. Be clear about where you are on your life's journey and what you need from a relationship. Clearly communicate why you need to make a change, using phrases such as, "Here's what I really need…"

Do not assign blame. Take responsibility for your role in ending the relationship and avoid calling attention to the other person's flaws. Share what you have learned from the relationship and what you're grateful for. Be appreciative, thankful, and be specific.

Create an opportunity for future reconciliation if appropriate because you never know what God may want to do later on, so avoid doing anything that would permanently prohibit the restoration of the relationship in some way at a later time. Lastly, let the person know you will continue to love him or her because the fact that a relationship is ending does not make the individual a bad or less-than person.

3. How do I respond to others when they ask why so-and-so and I aren't close anymore?

When you have been in a close relationship of any kind for a long time, whether personal or professional, people know it. When that relationship comes to an end, they will notice. The best way to respond if they ask about it is to say as little as possible, as positively as possible. For example, you can say something like, "Yeah, we don't spend as much time together anymore, but I think he or she is a great person," or "Well, we needed to go different directions based on the seasons of life that we both are in, but I sure did learn a lot from him or her."

When it's time to go and you gain clarity to determine that the relationship will no longer move forward with you, acknowledge the change. However, make that a minor point, while majoring on the positive points about the other person, because the relationship law of honor and loyalty applies even after a relationship ends.

Is it time to go in your relationship? At the end of the story, Barnabas so believes in John Mark and wants to help him that he leaves Paul in order to do so. The two cousins go on to do effective ministry. Paul chooses as his new colleague a man named Silas, who ultimately will co-author epistles with him, and who will be significant to Paul's next level of ministry. One way to look at this turn of events is to say that everyone involved ends up in the relationships they need to be in for their futures. You should also know that something positive happens between Paul and John Mark at some point.

My prayer for you is that this will be the case for you, like Paul and John Mark; that you will be able to move beyond good relationships gone bad and connect with people who will celebrate you, affirm you, and propel you into the future God has for you. The people in your life may change, but God's purpose for your life will not. Just as He sent Silas to Paul, in His grace, God will send you the right person for your future after you have had to let go of someone from your past, and you will go on to do great things. Is it time for your relationship to go?

CHAPTER 11

IT's Time to Say Goodbye!

The book of Ecclesiastes tells us that there is a time and a season for everything under the sun. This includes the area of relationships in our lives as sometimes, and quite often, we are faced with the reality of willfully saying farewell to former friendships for one reason or another. Is it time for you to say farewell to your relationship?

To fulfill the plan, purpose, and promise of God for your life, it will require a willingness and readiness to say goodbye to anything and everything that isn't willing to grow with you. The seasons and cycles of some things experienced in your life have expired, and the time is up to continue dealing with what you have already discerned, discovered, and determined is no longer good for you. Prior history is never the guarantee for future destiny.

Even if it's so hard to say goodbye to yesterday, today and what is to come are still awaiting you to do what you know in your spirit you need to do. Lift your hand and practice your wave, because some situations, dilemmas, obstacles, setbacks, stumbling blocks, tribulations, and circumstances are leaving your life for good, when you muster up the boldness and courage in the face of your fear and say goodbye to it.

I want to encourage you in this final chapter of *RelationShift* that the tears you cried for what was is becoming the joy you need for what now is, and is to come, in your life. What once was good and served its purpose is no longer satisfactory for this season, because when you release the old, you will experience and encounter the new. "Forget about what's happened; don't keep going over old history. Be alert, be present. I'm about to do something brand-new..." (Isa. 43:19, MSG).

To accelerate your life forward and faster, you can't continue dwelling on your past and the history, but you must focus on driving toward what's destined. Saying goodbye to some people, places, and things will transport you to what's ahead, but the vehicle God is using for you has limited seating that can only accommodate those who are willing to grow and go with you in the same direction.

Make up your mind and purpose in your heart to say goodbye to yesterday. What's gone is gone; what has happened has happened. Turn the page, pick yourself up, dust off your shoulders, apply the lesson learned, expect sweetness from the bitter experience, and move forward now. The past has died, the present is living, and the future is being born. This is your season to accelerate past your past on the interstate road of your life and on the journey of your story. This is because your past is continually trying to create further delays and make you drive slower than the speed limit assigned by God for your life to go.

Who and what do you need to say goodbye to today?

You can't go where God wants you to be until you say goodbye to where you are right now. Learning to recognize when something has run its course is a skill that will keep you moving forward, instead of trapped in things that have lost their value and purpose in your life. I pray that the Lord gives you a fresh set of eyes to see through the lenses of the lesson you learned, which becomes a preview and a glimpse of the greater that is in front of you. With this, you become blind to the bad things of your past that are still trying to haunt you. "Don't urge me to leave you or to turn back from you. Where you go I will go, and where you stay I will stay. Your people will be my people and your God my God" (Ruth 1:16. NIV).

God is not interested in fickleness; He is in love with faithfulness. It's easier to say goodbye when you aren't the only one leaving. The Lord is with you and has people for you. The Lord of your life is not looking at your past challenges; He's looking for a powerful and passionate commitment to move forward, with the trust you have in Him and the people He has assigned to walk with you. There are several relational lessons that can be learned from the story of Ruth, Naomi, and Orpah, but I want to focus on the fact that some people are created and intended to be companions in your calling and partners in your purpose; while other people will only commit to being halfway friends.

Everyone who comes into your life is not supposed to be a best friend, a member of your inner circle, or someone you trust with your hopes and fears or your joys and sadness. God brings long-term, deep, dependable friends into our lives, and He causes us to intersect with people who come into our lives for a specific reason or for a particular purpose. He sent Ruth into Naomi's to be a lifelong friend and covenant partner. Orpah was only in Naomi's life because she married Naomi's son. When he died, her season with Naomi came to an end. Her behavior provides a stark contrast to Ruth's fierce loyalty. Orpah's eventual willingness to leave Naomi is one of several reasons she is a halfway friend, not a covenant partner.

Failing to clearly understand the distinction between covenant partners and halfway friends has brought heartbreak and disappointment to many people. If we can understand and honor God's seasons and purposes for each relationship and connection, we and those with whom we relate to can enjoy blessing and fulfillment, within the context that God has ordained for our connections and commitments with others.

The question we should ask ourselves in the end, when we believe it is time to transition and exit from certain relationships, is this: What relationship should I say goodbye to? In the context of the story of Ruth, I want to provide you with five types of people or relationships you should say goodbye to:

1. People who refuse to change.
2. People who run away during difficulty.
3. People who rebel or resist your faith.
4. People who rebel your destiny decisions.
5. People who ruin your life.

In Ruth 1:6-15, notice that Naomi doesn't cling to Orpah; she doesn't beg her to stay and makes no effort to try to talk her out of it or entice her to go with them. She probably doesn't lose any sleep about the matter. The two women simply share a common, respectful parting gesture of their day and go their separate ways.

Orpah goes back to Moab, and very little, if anything, is ever written about her again. Ruth and Naomi travel on to Bethlehem, and a great story of restoration and redemption unfolds for both of them. Whenever you rebel against your opportunity of advancement and refuse to say goodbye to your past, nothing good and worth noting about your life will ever happen on purpose.

When a halfway friend decides to part ways with you, let that person go. When a season comes to an end, and you see the expiration date, let it go. Be assured that your destiny is never determined by any person who exits your life. There is nothing wrong with acknowledging the positive aspects of your acquaintance, and hopefully you will have the chance to wish the person well, but don't hold on to what may never happen.

You can't receive what God has planned, purposed, and promised you if you're holding on to who and what you need to let go of right now. If you are struggling in your soul to separate and sever a relationship that has expired in your season of life, remember these seven words to encourage and empower yourself: Yes, you will make it without them!

When a relationship and connection ends, one or both people involved may feel a bit unsteady for a while. Sometimes, a halfway friend will play mind games with you, saying, "I am going to leave," while also saying or insinuating, "and you'll never make it without me."

You may reflect on the qualities you grew to like in your halfway friend and ask yourself if you will make it without the person. Here is the answer to your internal question, with a resounding yes!.You will go through a transition period, as any necessary change happens, but I believe and pray that you will not only survive without the person/people, you will thrive.

If you don't say goodbye to the wrong people, you're providing them with the unearned blessing of your attention, which distracts you from focusing on who the right people are that God wants to welcome into your life.

There is no person who can prohibit your breakthrough and opportunity. The only person who can stop what God has for you is you. Whatever relationship tried to hold your life hostage, with your history together, is being broken so that your life can be free. Your responsibility is for your life, not for someone else's irresponsibility and immaturity. How long will you try to force what isn't happening? Do you want to experience the greater of God's goodness in your life? Is it time to say goodbye and farewell to an expired relationship?

I want to encourage you that you are not alone; everybody didn't walk away and all of them didn't leave. The right ones remain, and the wrong ones left. The right ones are still at your side right now. Fight for your forward focus, and don't forget your future because it's brighter than the darkness of your past. I rebuke and refuse to let the enemy have you tripping over people and over stuff that is behind you because it has nothing to do with your future. They cannot affect anything in front of you, because they no longer matter. Keep your eyes on the prize, and stay focused on the future, because our past was a set-up for the biggest comeback your circle of family and friends have ever seen. Whoever is still with you, cherish them, love on them, and don't make them pay for what those that left did to you. Treat people right, those who are still connected and still committed, and don't start looking at everybody like the enemy. God will show you Judas, but you won't be able to treat them differently because Judas still belongs to Jesus. God is teaching you how to love your enemy, even before they show you their real hand and identify themselves; it's called spiritual maturity and nothing that anyone has done will be powerful enough to stop what God has already planned, purposed, and promised you. This is because it's still your season to accelerate and move forward faster into what God has destined for you in Jesus's name!

CONCLUSION

RelationShift Me!

There is a recipe for right relationships where love wins over fear and peace, hope, and joy thrive. This recipe has three basic ingredients:

Connection: This is the goal in every healthy relationship. To be powerful in choosing this goal, we must overcome the fear that drives us to self-protect and choose distance with people.

Communication: To build and protect a healthy connection, we must become assertive communicators who vulnerably tell the truth about our thoughts, feelings, and needs and listen to understand and adjust.

Boundaries: To protect our relationships, we must establish healthy priorities and boundaries around ourselves and the levels of intimacy we nurture with each person.

RelationShift Declaration: I declare that God is establishing new seasons of growth and increase. I decree that I will be open to change, knowing that God has something better for me. New doors of opportunity, new partnerships, and new encounters of favor are in my present. Any relationship I have who sees no value in me is exiting my life and making room for those who will love me, appreciate my worth, and benefit from the hand of God on my life. Lord, you will surround me with people whose hearts are toward you and directed for me. In exchange of this blessing I receive, help me to be this very person to others. This is my RelationShift!

Prophetic Word: For this is the hour where you will know who's for you, with you, and not against you! When you come to the knowledge of My truth, you will be set free. I have neither called nor purposed for you to live out life alone, but you must know those that are to remain in your life for that which I am doing in your life can only be handled by those who are not intimidated by your life. Some people have turned against you and walked away without reason, and IT has nothing to do with you personally. IT is because I have removed them from your life because they cannot go where I am leading you next. If I permitted them to remain, they would hinder you at the next place, because they have already served their purpose in your life. Determine truthfully today to let them go and keep moving forward toward My greater that I have prepared for you that is coming your way. Where I am calling you, everyone you know can't go. My anointing on your life will cause a separation from anyone that hinders your obedience to Me.

1 John 2:19 (NKJV) "They went out from us, but they were not of us; for if they had been of us, they would have continued with us; but they went out that they might be made manifest, that none of them were of us."

This is your RelationShift!

Notes

Scripture Quotations (Bible Translations Used): NIV, NKJV, NLT, AMP, MSG

Dharius Daniels, *Re-Present Jesus* (Lake Mary, FL: Charisma House Book Group, 2014).

Stephen M.R. Covey, *The Speed of Trust* (New York, NY: Free Press, 2006, 2018).

Vanable H. Moody II, *The People Factor* (Nashville, TN: Nelson Books, 2014).

Cover Design By: Shalondie Stephen & Lamar Harvey

Author Photo: Lamar T. Harvey

CPSIA information can be obtained
at www.ICGtesting.com
Printed in the USA
FFHW022317120419
51728840-57148FF

9 781545 664995